# JACKSON HOLE

# A Sport Climbing
# and
# Bouldering Guide

by Joe Sottile

Pingora Press
Post Office Box 6657
Bozeman, Montana
59715

Sottile, Joe
Jackson Hole : A Sport Climbing
and Bouldering Guide /
Joe Sottile.—2nd ed.

1st edition titled Full Circle
Copyright © 1991

ISBN 0-9632396-1-9
1. Sottile, Joe, 1953—
3rd Edition
*May 1994*

This book was set in 12/14 Times Roman
Text in Word Perfect 5.1®
Page layout was created in PageMaker 4.0® for Windows®
All scans with Logitech's Scanman 256®
Camera-ready copy produced with the HP Laser Jet IIIP®
Overall production accomplished on a 386sx PC.

*Front Cover: Marjean Heisler on Time Flies While You're Alive,*
*Blacktail Butte*
*Back Cover: Nancy Feagin on Electric Shower,*
*Hoback Shield*
*Title Page: Max Yanoff on Section V at Badger Creek,*
*photo by Marjean Heisler*
*All uncredited photos by the author*

*Once again, for Marjean*

## Warning

This is a guidebook to a potentially dangerous activity. It is not intended for use as an instruction manual and should not be regarded as a substitute for sound judgement. Rock climbing, by its very nature, is a high risk sport, and the reader hereby releases the author, publisher, and distributors of *Jackson Hole: A Sport Climbing and Bouldering Guide* from liability for any injury, including death, that might result.

# *Preface*

*"The spirit of the valley never dies. "*
*-Lao Tzu from the* Tao Te Ching

F IRST, I WOULD LIKE TO THANK EVERYONE who chose to purchase the first edition of *Full Circle*. Voting with one's dollars is the most convincing and flattering kind of support. I hope the second edition is met with equal enthusiasm and is of even greater value. I've incorporated many suggestions from owners of the 1991 guide and have eliminated much of the nonsense I mistook for wisdom in the first edition.

**A Notable Addition** is the brief descriptive text associated with all the major crags and bouldering areas. **Entirely New** information includes: topos and text of a new sport area known as The Tram in Teton Village, topos and extended text on the Badger Creek, Boulder City and Jenny Lake boulders. **Brand New** information is given on two small crags in nearby Idaho, and, of course, all new routes put up at the established cliffs since the first edition. **Another New Feature** is the glossary to help the newcomer navigate the alien and truncated conversations that are sometimes associated with the sport. By no means is it comprehensive, primarily because of regional specificity and the ephemeral nature of jargon, but it should serve one well when being offered essential *beta*. I've tried to keep descriptive text to a minimum, for your benefit as well as mine, and have drawn topos to include only salient and orienting features. **There Is Also** a regional reading list of varied topics covering northwestern Wyoming.

# *Acknowledgments*

*"You know what I think is most important in this world?*
*Friends, that's what I think..."*
-from the movie , Fried Green Tomatoes

JAMES A. MICHENER SAID in his memoirs, *The World is My Home*, that he figured at least thirty different people proof-read his manuscript before it ever went to the presses. Even so, soon after picking up a store copy he immediately discovered at least five misspelled words—I should be so fortunate. Along with spelling, my chief concerns were consistency, accuracy and readability. To ensure and maintain that criteria, I had the assistance of a number of thoughtful and conscientious individuals. Aimee Barnes, in her delightful and refreshing directness, ferreted out a number of glossary inaccuracies, as well as pointing out the absence of a wonderful route I neglected to include in the Grand Wall topo. I wish to thank Judy Eddy for her key instruction in *PageMaker* (In the beginning, I had trouble discerning which way was up). She is also an extraordinary reference, expert grammarian and made more than a few suggestions that elevated the manuscript a full letter grade in maturity. Sharon Gilchrist snatched me from the jaws of profound embarrassment with suggestions on design and page layout. Paula McDougal, whose assistance was invaluable in the first edition, once again proved that attention to detail is a most important element and one of the more easily overlooked aspects of a project as it nears its completion. Her suggestions on balance and style improved the presentation considerably and her knowledge of the production process eliminated many of my pre-press anxieties.

I would also like to extend my gratitude to those who offered suggestions and corrections regarding route information. These generous individuals include: Jim Woodmency for suggestions on Boulder Island Boulder and the Corral Boulder, Jim Howe for updates on the Upper Blacktail crag, Chuck Odett for route info on Heise and Paramount, and Greg Miles and Rich Collins for new route information in S&S and Corbet's Couloirs.

Any faux pas, social or otherwise, design flaws, grammatical errors, awkward sentence structure etc., I take full responsibility. They either slipped through the cracks in the deadline rush (you know, when you can barely spell your *own* name correctly), or, I was characteristically stubborn and neglected the wise counsel of my editing team.

Aside from the technical aspects of this work, and be assured I value it no less, I want to thank the many individuals who supported me during a crisis of job termination which necessitated relocation and thus separation from my friends and community of thirteen years. Those people were instrumental in their support when my confidence was low, and were significant in the fact that this book, indeed, is available and on time.

And finally, to the one who needed to tolerate my neurosis, indecisions, alpine starts on new chapters and downright irritability and childishness, I must thank Marjean. Her support was enduring and comprehensive; from trips to the library to trips to the crags. She was stable when I was not. She was softly encouraging when the doldrums struck.

the author

# Contents

# *Introduction*

Luddite 1. a member of an 18th century group who organized to destroy machinery in the belief that machines would cause the loss of their jobs. 2. Modern day euphemism for someone who is inordinately opposed to change.

S PORT CLIMBING HAS BROKEN the psychological barrier of what was once considered technically attainable in free rock climbing. The Salathé goes free, speed ascents of the Nose are made and long free ascents are quickly dispatched in the Himalaya. It is no coincidence that the people involved in these admirable accomplishments had in their broad experience strong sport climbing development.

This is not to say that someone who can clip 5.12 on the valley floor is going to be able to do the same at 12,000 feet in a pair of plastic boots while placing natural protection. That would be a frightening, indirect, and illogical assessment. There is no substitute for proper instruction and extensive mountaineering experience. But the strength, power, balance and technique gained from working difficult sport routes is certainly going to serve one well when combined with the necessary mountaineering skills. This is where the Tetons and Jackson Hole demonstrate, in bold strokes, their continual role in the forefront of American climbing. Nowhere else in the world, except perhaps Chamonix, is there quality bouldering, excellent sport climbing and world class mountaineering within such proximity of one another. An environment this rich, that allows convenient integration of all aspects of the sport, will enable us to develop the many disciplines necessary to push the limits in mountaineering.

Paul Piana refers to short sport routes as haikus, which can be woven into an epic work—if one chooses. With this approach in mind, it appears the Tetons are going to begin to see some exciting new free ascents. I suspect the first free solo ascent of the North Face of the Grand by Alex Lowe in the winter of '91—'92, and the second free ascent of The Sunshine Dihedral in the summer of '91 by John McMullen and Clint Harbor, will come to be recognized as some of the first climbs to represent this new standard of alpine ascent. These successes underscore the value of sport climbing in the larger context of mountaineering.

Sport climbing's detractors have said that it is the 'bastard of rock climbing.' Besides being insensitive, this myopic view simply misses the point. Such philistine attitudes have rarely been responsible for allowing visionary ideas or activities to reach their full potential. To be sure, some violations have occurred. The popularity of sport climbing has led, on occasion, to property abuses and the attending problems of overuse. These considerations in of themselves hardly make sport climbing unique. One only needs to look at the landfill project at the Everest basecamp for clarification of this argument. It is also important to understand, to a large extent, we are *all* to blame for these offenses—whatever outdoor activity we pursue. So in this light, to isolate sport climbing and dismiss it entirely because of the actions of a few, is an unexamined perspective at best.

•　　•　　•

At this point in the introduction readers begin looking for the names of people who put up this and that climb, discovered this and that crag, flashed this or that route. I'm going to maintain the sport climbing tradition and dispense with a 'who's who' of first ascents, route development, first redpoints, etc. Instead, I'd like to extend my appreciation to all of you who had the courage and vision to bolt the toprope lines against the din of naysayers. For everyone who has spent time and money retrobolting unsafe routes, improving anchors and replacing pins, thank you for your outstanding generosity and consideration of others. And for those of you exploring new cliffs and developing routes at all grades, thanks for helping to keep this sport from becoming elitist and arrogant by virtue of a 'hard route only' criteria.

In all fairness, people with drills and/or those who climb 5.12 are not the only players here. The activity is replete with people of many talents and persuasion: those who understand trail maintenance, those who choose to instruct, those who guide and others who maintain organizations like the American Alpine Club, Friends of the City and The Access Fund. All of these people who are active, internally or peripherally, contribute to the growing popularity and continual development of sport climbing and climbing in general. To all of you, in every aspect of the genre, I want to express my gratitude for your efforts.

Apart from this, I've always felt the beauty of sport climbing lies in its utterly social and indiscriminate nature. As one travels the crags you meet the young, the old, male, female, expert and neophyte. It is a rich environment where meeting new people is easy and most often enlightening, and this in a time of great disparity and compartmentalization, is a boon. Whoever thought the sense of a community could be garnered at the crags? Armed with such insight, maybe we begin to realize that ticking off the grades isn't all that important, and for some, not important at all.

Joe Suttilo
Bozeman, Montana
1994

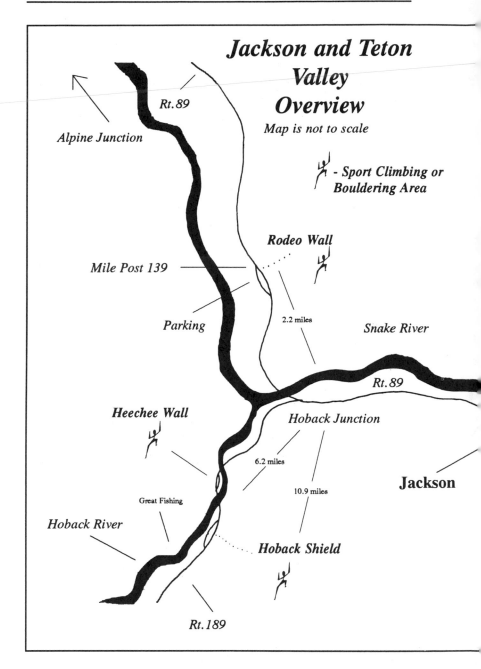

# Jackson and Teton Valley Overview

*Map is not to scale*

- Sport Climbing or Bouldering Area

Rt. 89

Alpine Junction

Rodeo Wall

Mile Post 139

Parking

2.2 miles

Snake River

Rt. 89

Heechee Wall

Hoback Junction

6.2 miles

10.9 miles

Jackson

Great Fishing

Hoback River

Hoback Shield

Rt. 189

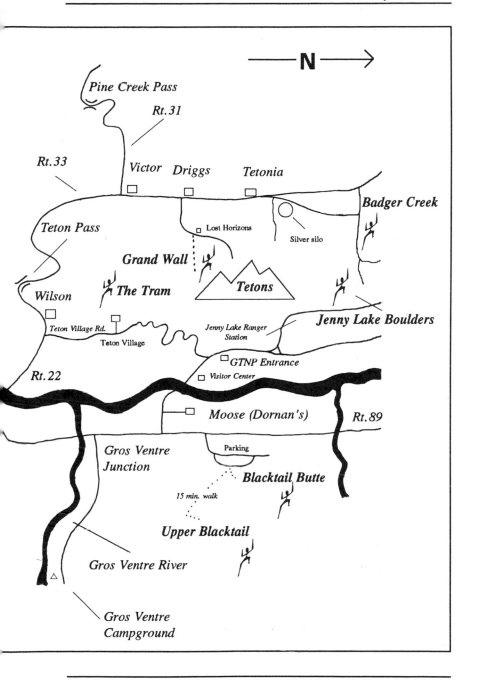

# *Legend*

| | |
|---|---|
| Natural belay | ◯ |
| Bolt belay | ⊗ |
| Route of ascent | • • • • • • |
| Bolt | **X** |
| Piton/Fixed pin | **FP** |
| Roof/Overhang | ▭ / ⊔⊔⊔⊔⊔ |
| Straight-in-crack | \| — |
| Right-facing corner | |
| Left-facing corner | |
| Natural pro needed | ✳ |
| Questionable protection or few placements available | r |

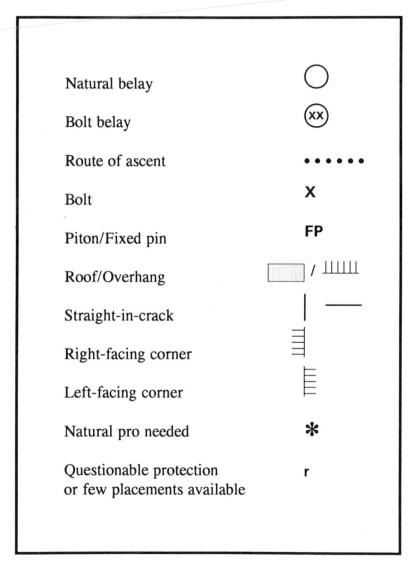

# About Putting All Those Damn Bolts In...

*"Nothing great was ever accomplished
without enthusiasm. "*
*-Ralph Waldo Emerson*

**M**OST ROUTES IN THE AREA have been toproped before bolting to ensure challenging, yet safe route character. Standard hardware is at least 3/8 x 31/2 inch Rawl bolt or equivalent. My feeling at this time, considering the ubiquitous nature of the power drill and the extraordinary traffic sport routes enjoy, is that 1/2 inch diameter bolts seem to be the wiser choice. Another reason to go with 1/2 inch is the relatively low torque recommendation for 3/8 inch. At only 35 lbs., a bolt can be easily overtorqued using a ratchet. At the very least, the bolt head shears off in your hand during placement. At worst, the bolt head pops at the next severe fall. At 60 lbs. for 1/2 inch, overtorquing is unlikely. In *Climbing* magazine, issues #134 and #135 there are two outstanding articles by Duane Raliegh. They cover bolt types, placement technique and preferred medium. When Mr. Raliegh writes articles of this quality, he simply has no peers.

Anchors, for the most part, are two 3/8 x 31/2 inch bolts equipped with 3/8 inch chain. Allen Sanderson, with remarkable thoroughness, covers this topic very well in *Climbing* magazine, August/September 1990, issue #191. Try to keep new routes at this high standard until new technology proves otherwise, and whenever possible, please refrain from establishing r and x* routes.

Technical proficiency, although essential, is only one as-

* injury or death in the event of a fall

pect of the ability to establish quality sport routes. Assessing sound rock, choosing an esthetic line and ensuring that the route is a safe lead, are only a few of the myriad considerations that need to be taken into account when establishing a climb. I like to think of route building as akin to road building: it should have easy access, a nice view, be able to withstand heavy traffic and be safe at most reasonable speeds. Ric Lince covers this topic in much more detail in *The Connection*, June/July 1991. The name of the article is 'Do the Right Thing' and the sub-title reads, 'Stop-Think-Reconsider'. Sounds pretty straightforward to me.

Regarding local ethics and the development of new routes,* there has been no consensus as far as I know, and I certainly will not patronize and suggest what is politically correct in this region. I do think the emphasis should be on safety, and that is as much as I would like to say on the subject. Unfortunately, no matter how thoughtful and intelligent your route may be, someone will manage to disagree, and as noted in the topo diagrams, some chopping has occured.

---

* in areas outside GTNP and designated Primitive and Wilderness areas; otherwise, please check with appropriate agencies.

---

# Grand Wall

*"What were once only local demoralizations or disasters now threaten to turn into planetary calamities."*
*-from* The Condition of Man *by Lewis Mumford*

G RAND WALL IS A LARGE and glacially polished granite monolith on the west side of the Tetons. It has quite an assortment of long sport climbs (eighteen clips!), and is the home of the severely overhanging and cervically distorting testpiece known as Arms Deal, 5.13a (wear jeans for the knee-lock). The easiest route here is 5.9, with most climbs in the hard 5.11 to easy 5.12 range. One rope is all that is needed. You can walk off either side of the formation.

Grand Wall lies just within the boundary of designated Wilderness, and I was asked to relay to all concerned that permanent fixtures and power tools are prohibited in these areas.

**Getting There:** Follow US 22 over Teton Pass and into Driggs, Idaho. At the main intersection turn right (east) following signs for Grand Targhee Ski Resort. After 5.9 miles, Lost Horizons Restaurant will be on your left. Turn right into Teton Canyon and continue until you reach the trailhead and can drive no further. Follow the well-maintained trail east for a few minutes. The formation appears immediately on your left, to the north. This is also the trailhead for Devil's Staircase and Table Mountain; two delightful day hikes, I've been told. For those of you who enjoy long division, the Grand can be climbed from here as well.

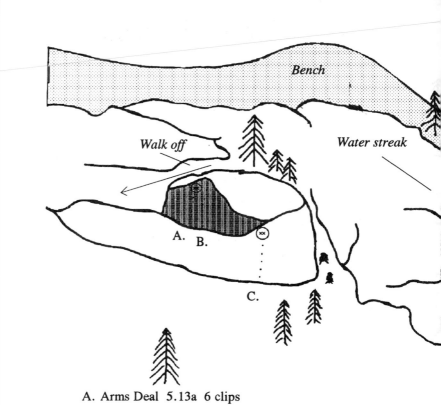

A. Arms Deal  5.13a  6 clips
B. Munger Crack  5.11c  natural pro
C. Dr. Hole  5.12a
D. Ladykiller  5.11a  natural pro start
E. Bambi  5.11a
F. Thumper  5.11b
G. S.O.S.  5.10d
H. Mayday  5.12a  18 clips
I.  High Noon  5.12a  16 clips
J.  Afternoon Delight  5.12a/b  17 clips
K. Uki-Waza 'floating technique'  5.12a
L. Kin-Jite 'forbidden subject'  5.11d
M. Ninjitsu  5.11c
N. Z-Crack 5.9+  natural pro

# Grand Wall

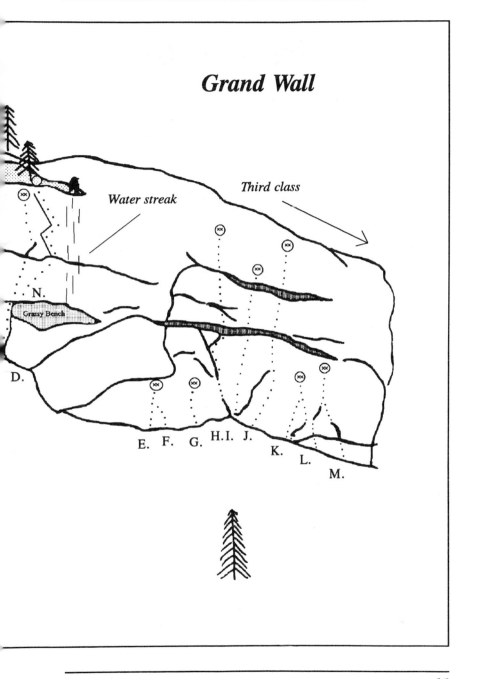

Water streak

Third class

N.

Grassy Bench

D.

E. F. G. H.I. J.

K.

L.

M.

# Blacktail Butte

*"Those of us who can best endure the good and evil*
*of life have the best education. "*
*- Jean-Jacques Rousseau*

O NE COULD ARGUE THAT THE CLIMBING which developed at Blacktail Butte was the precursor to sport
climbing in Jackson Hole. For years, this crag boasted the
testpiece toprope problems in the region. Then in the late 80's
the cliff started to see a few bolted lines. Of course this made
a few people unhappy, but it soon became clear that if people
wanted to break into 5.12 climbing they were going to need
reasonable access to safe routes in that grade. Overnight,
Blacktail Butte saw a tremendous amount of attention, and,
indeed, many people began to realize the elusive 5.12.

The consistent difficulty and highly technical nature of
the routes at this limestone formation is determined by small
and micro edges on a slightly greater than vertical face. Most
leadable routes are clip-ups, with the exceptions being The
Raven Crack and The Diagonal Crack. The Diagonal Crack
was initially led with natural protection and was considered
a very serious lead. The route was bolted in the fall of 1990
and saw numerous ascents. In the spring of 1991 it was
chopped. See what you think.

**Getting There:** Drive north of Jackson on Rt. 89 for 12 miles,
passing Moose Junction (entrance to GTNP) on your left.
Turn at the next right and enter the parking lot. Walk directly
east, following the unmaintained trail upwards through loose
limestone talus, passing a long B1 + traverse immediately on
your left. After a few minutes you arrive at the main cliff,

characterized by the seemingly blank and vertical south face.

To reach the Upper Blacktail cliffs, leave the south end of the parking lot and gain the horse trail that traverses the base of the butte in a southeasterly direction. After fifteen minutes or so, limestone talus from above on your left reaches the trail. At this point, traverse up and left, over the talus, to reach the lower of the two cliffs. The larger cliff is directly behind. This is a great place to go if the roadside cliff is crowded, or, if your fingers need a rest from those micro edges. Although these cliffs are composed of limestone as well, their hold character varies greatly from the main crag below. This area features a number of pocket-pulling routes in the easy to hard 5.11 range—well worth the hike.

*The main lower cliff of Blacktail Butte*
*as seen from Rt. 89*

# Blacktail Butte

A. As You Wish 5.11b
B. Inconcievable 5.11a
C. Do the Right Thing 5.11d
D. Water Streak Direct 5.13a
E. Water Streak 5.12b
F. Arch Direct 5.12b
G. The Arch 5.12a
H. Bolt Route 5.11a
I. Jingus Road 5.12a
J. Diagonal Crack 5.11a,r* (chopped)
K. Time Flies While You're Alive 5.10c
L. Kehoe Kling 5.12b
M. Your Route 5.12b
N. Breashear's Route 5.12b
O. Monster Route 5.13a, variation
P. Right Crack 5.9
Q. Connect 5.12a, variation
R. The Squeeze 5.12c, variation
S. Raven Crack 5.9*
   natural pro

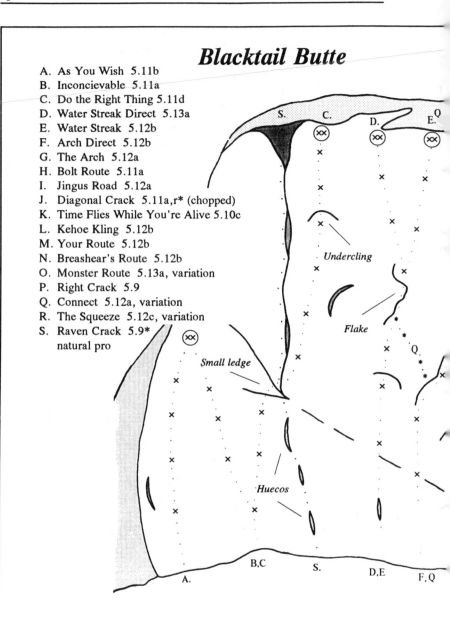

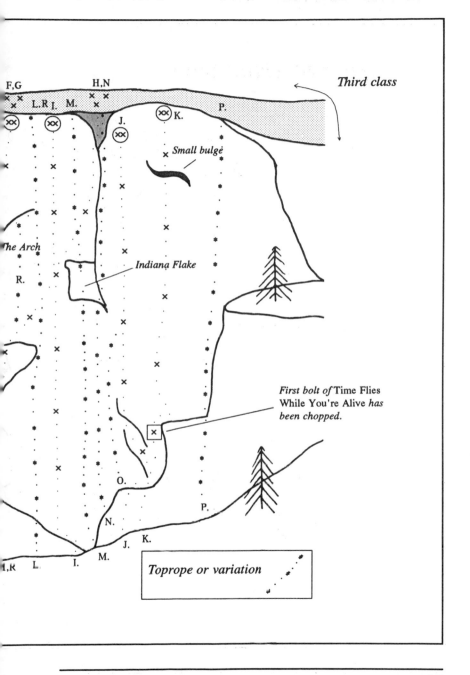

Third class

F,G

H,N

L.R I. M.

J.

K.

P.

× Small bulge

he Arch

R.

*Indiana Flake*

First bolt *of* Time Flies While You're Alive *has been chopped.*

O.

P.

N.

K.

1,R    L.    I.    M.    J.

*Toprope or variation*

# Upper Blacktail Butte

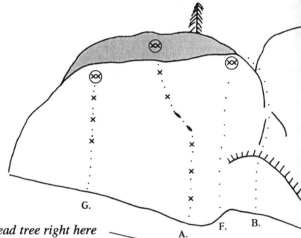

G.

*Fallen dead tree right here* ——————

A.

F.  B.

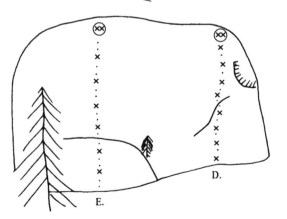

D.

E.

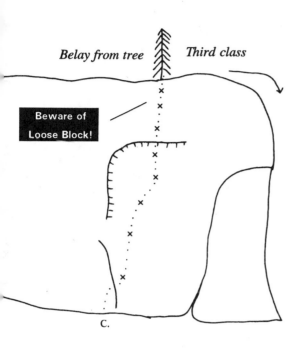

*Belay from tree*    *Third class*

**Beware of Loose Block!**

C.

A. Graceland  5.11b 6 clips
B. Garden of Screamin'  5.10r natural pro
C. Wild at Heart  5.11b  8 clips
D. Muy Macho 5.10d  7 clips
E. Blitzkrieg  5.11d  6 clips
F. Project
G.    ?        5.12a  runout to first clip

# *Hoback Shield*

*In 1946 journalist David Schoenbrun asked Ho Chi Minh, "If the
French do not give you some form of independence,
President Ho, what will you do?"
"Why we will fight, of course," said Ho.
-from* Ho, *by David Halberstam*

THIS LIMESTONE CRAG OFFERS the most variety in the moderate to easy grades. Located 10.9 miles south of the Hoback Junction on Rt. 189, this cliff's selection of routes range from a 5.5 toprope to a 5.11b face route which includes a significant roof as well. The Shield is characterized by a long arching roof system and most routes are clip-ups with 3/8 inch chain anchors. Natural pro routes are noted in the topos. A standard rack to a 3.5 Friend is recommended gear for the natural pro routes and a dozen quickdraws will see you through all of the bolted lines. Climbers should take note that the upper pitches are generally loose, except for the second pitch of Electric Shower and Deception. A few topropes can be reached by walking up the ramp on the right side of the crag. A 5.5 traverse from the end of the ramp will allow one to reach the anchors on Deception. Because of the loose nature of the rock, it is not recommended that you access the anchors from above. Climb at the Hoback Shield in the morning, and by noon on a sunny day you'll be scrambling for the Hoback River below. At about 2 in the afternoon, make your way to Rodeo Wall, which will be going into shade about then.

**Getting There:** Drive south out of Jackson on Rt. 89 for approximately 12 miles to Hoback Junction. Bear left at Hoback Junction on Rt. 189 and continue for 10.9 miles. Here you will see a pull-out on your right, beside the Hoback River.

*The Hoback Shield as seen from the south side of the Hoback River.*

If pull-out is crowded, continue another quarter of a mile and park just after the bridge on the right-hand side of the road, across from Battle Mountain Lodge.

The stretch of river from the bridge downstream can offer some excellent fly fishing just before and after spring run-off. The boating is excellent here as well, and both offer opportunities to cool off during the mid-day sun.

*Nancy Feagin pulls the roof on* Electric Shower.

# *Hoback Shield*

A. Toprope  5.8
B. Petzle Logic  5.10c
C. A Thousand Cranes  5.9
D. The Joker  5.10a
E. Malvado Edge  5.8, 5.9*
F. Muffbuster  5.10c, 5.9*
G. Electric Shower  5.11b, 5.10c
H. Toprope  5.12b
I. She's Gotta Have It!  5.10c
J. Dengue Fever  5.10d
K. Fandango  5.10c* small nuts
L. The Hunter  5.9r*

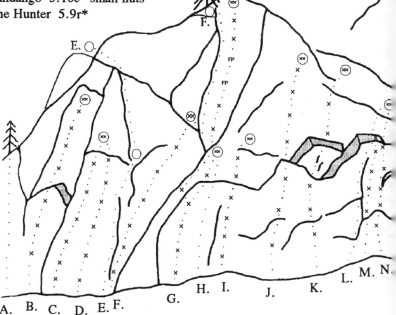

*Third class*

M. Naughty Guides  5.10a
N. La Bamba  5.10a
O. Mc Flatus Roof  5.10c*
P. Nhervus Sheep Direct  5.11b
Q. Nhervus Sheep  5.11a
R. The Bulge  5.8, 5.10a*
S. Deception  5.10c, 5.8*

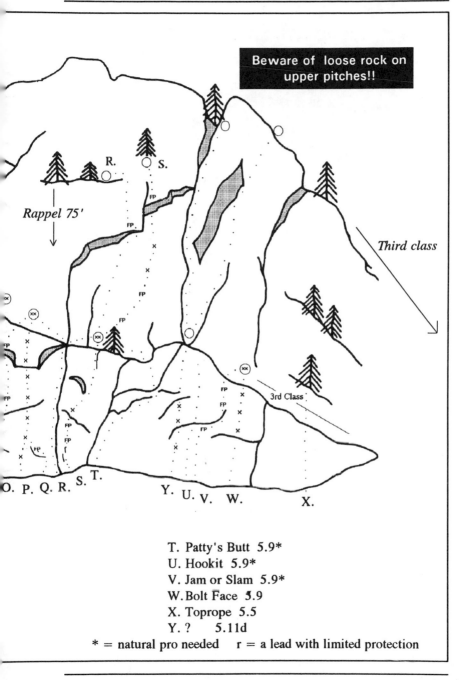

Beware of loose rock on upper pitches!!

Rappel 75'

R.    S.

Third class

3rd Class

O. P. Q. R. S. T.    Y. U. V. W.    X.

T. Patty's Butt  5.9*
U. Hookit  5.9*
V. Jam or Slam  5.9*
W. Bolt Face  5.9
X. Toprope  5.5
Y. ?    5.11d
* = natural pro needed    r = a lead with limited protection

*Rodeo Wall from the roadside of Rt. 89*

# *Rodeo Wall*

*"Free at last, free at last, thank God Almighty, free at last."*
*-Martin Luther King, Jr.*

*"One out of twenty-one Black American males will be murdered in their lifetime."*
*-from the introduction to the movie* Boyz-n-the-Hood

I N THE SUMMER OF 1991, Rodeo Wall made a spirited attack on The Hoback Shield's enduring popularity. The reasons are quite obvious. First, although there are fewer routes at Rodeo Wall, they all demonstrate an excellent quality of line and are intelligently bolted. Second, the near vertical limestone crag lent itself to an interesting erosional process that left behind patches of brown patina which serve as excellent edges. Some routes reveal a few shallow pockets as well. And last, is the fact that Rodeo goes in shade at about 2 in the afternoon during the summer months. So as your feet bake, and that new resole job is melting before your eyes while at the Hoback Shield, think of heading to the Rodeo in the early afternoon. Late 1991 additions to Rodeo Wall are Thelma & Louise rated 5.9 and 5.10a, respectively.

**Getting There:** Head south from Jackson on Rt.89 and at Hoback Junction, bear right on Rt.89 entering the Snake River Canyon. Two and two-tenths miles beyond Hoback Junction, park at the 139 mile marker, which appears on your left. Crag is the obvious formation across the road, to the north.

# Rodeo Wall

*All routes here are clip-ups!*

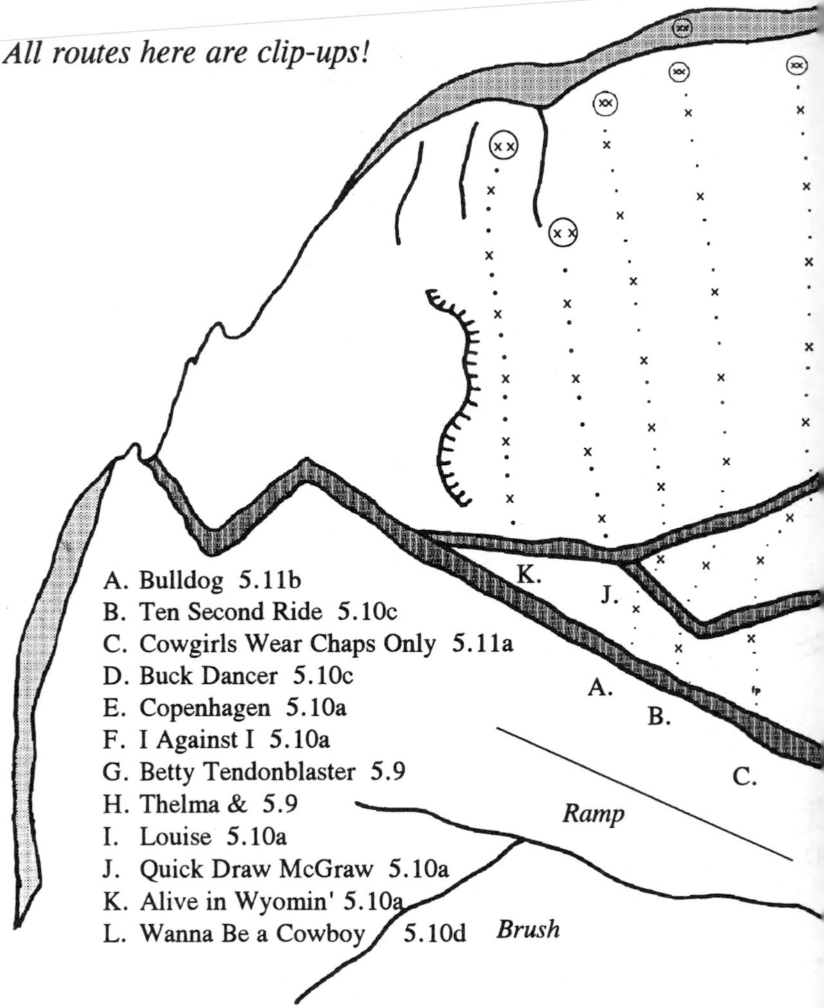

A. Bulldog 5.11b
B. Ten Second Ride 5.10c
C. Cowgirls Wear Chaps Only 5.11a
D. Buck Dancer 5.10c
E. Copenhagen 5.10a
F. I Against I 5.10a
G. Betty Tendonblaster 5.9
H. Thelma & 5.9
I. Louise 5.10a
J. Quick Draw McGraw 5.10a
K. Alive in Wyomin' 5.10a
L. Wanna Be a Cowboy 5.10d

K.

J.

A.

B.

C.

*Ramp*

*Brush*

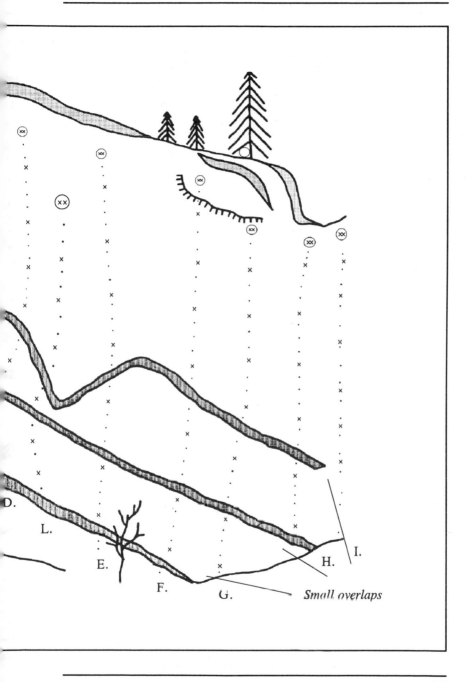

L.

D.

E.

F.

G.

H.

I.

Small overlaps

# *Heechee Wall*

*"But who could handle such a thing? It was a hydra, merciless and uncontrolable, and it was Landau's image for turbulence: infinite modes, infinite degrees of freedom, infinite dimensions. "*
*-from  James Gleick's* Chaos: Making a New Science

S IX MILES SOUTH OF HOBACK JUNCTION, just beyond the Stinking Springs turnout on Rt.189, lies a parking area on the north side of the road. Across the road (south) and fifteen minutes up limestone talus, is the little-known Heechee Wall. This vertical limestone cliff has one route with clear potential for others in its grade. Rumor has it a visiting lifeform established the six clip climb during the plethora of UFO sightings during the 1930s. Oral history gives the existing route a rating of 5.12b, with a challenging second clip (lengthy extraterrestial limbs?). The route's name, Easy Travel to Other Planets, suggests a walk-up for the early ascensionists.

# The Tram

## Corbet's and S&S Couloirs

*"Governing a large state is like boiling a small fish."*
*-Lao Tzu in the* Tao Te Ching

I F YOU HAVE BEEN IN JACKSON HOLE long enough, you have probably seen the ad stating 'Ride the Aerial Tram to the Top of the Tetons.' The ad purports that one is taken to the heart of the Tetons. Well, that is not entirely true. What the ad doesn't say, but, in fact is absolutely true, is that there is some excellent sport climbing near the top of the tram on steep, pocketed, well protected dolomite. This is the place to be on days when the valley floor is sweltering.

**Getting There:** Once you've arrived at Teton Village and are at the base of the Watch Tower, you can walk to the cliff. Yeah, right. Or, you can purchase one round trip ride for the outrageous fee of $13.00 for visitors, $6.00 for people with local I.D. This is sport climbing in the mountains. Be sure to take along additional clothing as well as effective sunblock. A tank top and crop tights could leave your teeth chattering if you fail to catch the last tram. Check the current schedule. A fate worse than death, namely embarrassment, awaits one if benighted on a sport climb. Once you disembark the tram, walk south for a few minutes to the bulletin board overview map. Bear left here (east) and follow the trail downwards with the tram cables on your left. Five minutes walking brings you to the first of two gullies distinguished by out-of-bounds signs. The first gully is Corbet's Couloir whose east face is clearly recognized by the predominence of water stain. Access the routes fourth class via the the gully or rap (125 ft.)

from anchors above routes Sky Pilot or Nature Hike. The second gully is S&S Couloir and routes are reached by rappeling (75 ft.) from the anchors above Shadow Silence. Medium sized protection is recommended at these belays because, much like the condominiums below, space is at a premium, though slightly less costly.

*Kevin Patno at the start of* Ravin' Roof Bypass *in Corbet's Couloir-East.*

A. Shadow Silence  5.10b - lg. stopper
B. New World  5.10c - #1 Friend
C. Fire in the Hole  5.10c
D. High Boltage  5.7 - #s 1,2, and 2.5 Friends for traverse

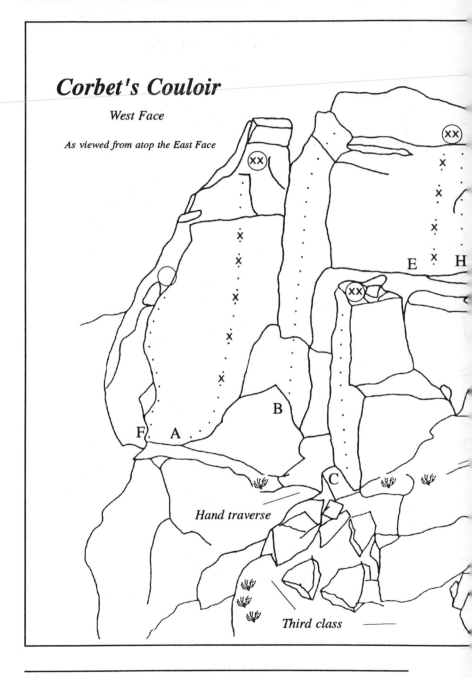

## Corbet's Couloir

*West Face*

*As viewed from atop the East Face*

E   H

B

F   A

C

*Hand traverse*

*Third class*

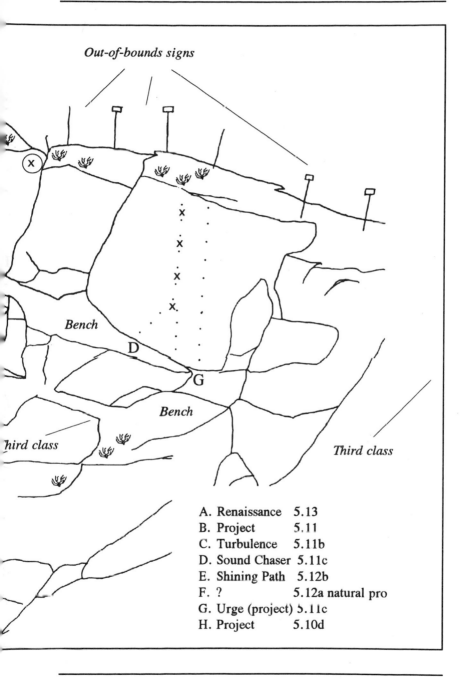

Out-of-bounds signs

Bench

D

G

Bench

hird class

Third class

A. Renaissance 5.13
B. Project 5.11
C. Turbulence 5.11b
D. Sound Chaser 5.11c
E. Shining Path 5.12b
F. ? 5.12a natural pro
G. Urge (project) 5.11c
H. Project 5.10d

# Corbet's Couloir

## East Face

*As viewed from atop the West Face*

Third class

Third class

Third class

Water-stained face

Loose, sandy scree

A

B

C

D

E

F

G

Bench

Roof

A. Saxifrage  5.9
B. Grey-Crowned Cracks  5.9 natural pro
C. Harebell  5.11b
D. Sky Pilot  5.11c
E. Nature Hike  5.10d

F. Ravin' Roof Bypass  5.12a, 11b if you eliminate boulder move at the top.
G. Ravin' Roof  5.12 - Tape and a #1.5 Friend are handy for the roof crack.

# Heise and Paramount

*"Let's be clear. The planet is not in jeopardy. We are in jeopardy. "*
*-Ian Malcolm in* Jurassic Park *by Michael Crichton*

T HE TETONS, BLACKTAIL BUTTE  and the Hoback Shield
are quite enjoyable, but a climbing trip to the West would
not be complete without a few days at the City of Rocks. No,
I'm not going to do a chapter on the City. Dave Bingham's
latest effort on the area is thoughtful and comprehensive. This
is about a little known area outside of Idaho Falls which is
easily reached on your way to the City, *and* is near the
delightful hot springs of Heise. Thirty routes are offered,
most of which are clip-ups, with noted exceptions. The first
formation is the Heise Boulder located just beyond the
soothing Heise Hot Springs. This large boulder, of approximately 40 feet high, has fifteen developed routes ranging
from 5.7 to 5.12d. The second formation, known as Paramount, is composed of an interesting volcanic substance, and
has many delightful routes in the 5.8 to 5.10 range. Chuck
and Jed's Excellent Adventure is a superb 5.8 fist crack and
comes highly recommended as a natural pro line.

**Getting There:** With a bagel in one hand and a latté in the
other, drive over Teton Pass to Victor. In Victor, turn left on
Rt.31 and continue to Swan Valley. In Swan Valley, turn
right toward Idaho Falls and after 23.5 miles turn right
following the signs to Heise Hot Springs. One-half mile past
the Springs, on your left, is the Heise Boulder. Another 1.5
miles on your left is the Paramount formation, at the mouth
of Kelly Canyon.

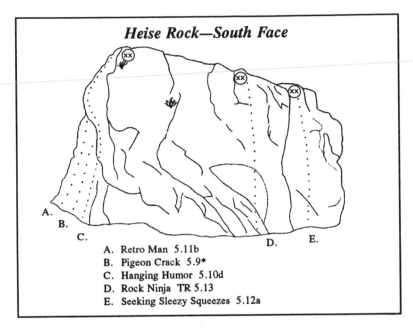

# Heise Rock—South Face

A.
B.
C.
D.    E.

A. Retro Man  5.11b
B. Pigeon Crack  5.9*
C. Hanging Humor  5.10d
D. Rock Ninja  TR 5.13
E. Seeking Sleezy Squeezes  5.12a

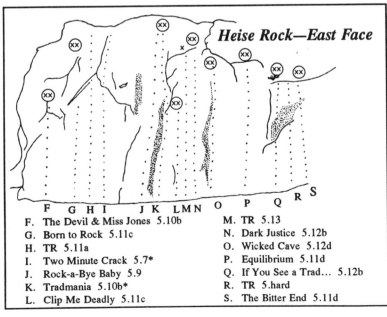

## Heise Rock—East Face

F    G  H  I      J K   L M N   O    P    Q    R  S

F. The Devil & Miss Jones  5.10b
G. Born to Rock  5.11c
H. TR  5.11a
I. Two Minute Crack  5.7*
J. Rock-a-Bye Baby  5.9
K. Tradmania  5.10b*
L. Clip Me Deadly  5.11c

M. TR  5.13
N. Dark Justice  5.12b
O. Wicked Cave  5.12d
P. Equilibrium  5.11d
Q. If You See a Trad...  5.12b
R. TR  5.hard
S. The Bitter End  5.11d

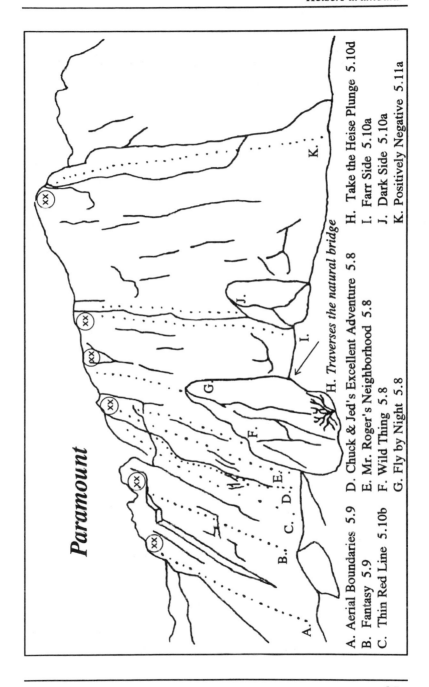

*Paramount*

A. Aerial Boundaries 5.9   D. Chuck & Jed's Excellent Adventure 5.8   H. Take the Heise Plunge 5.10d
B. Fantasy 5.9              E. Mr. Roger's Neighborhood 5.8                I. Farr Side 5.10a
C. Thin Red Line 5.10b     F. Wild Thing 5.8                              J. Dark Side 5.10a
                           G. Fly by Night 5.8                            K. Positively Negative 5.11a

H. *Traverses the natural bridge*

# *Note on Bouldering*

*"Standards are wonderful. Let's have a hundred of them!"*
*-Anonymous*

**B**OULDERING BUILDS STRENGTH, endurance, power and confidence. It is also a leading cause of chronic and acute injury to the connective tissues and bony structures of the hand and ankle. Please be sure to stretch, warm up and proceed slowly before attempting problems at your limit. Although none of the bouldering areas in this region would be listed in the top ten, combined they offer tremendous variety and opportunity. Bouldering's beauty lies in its simplicity. Shoes, chalk and a tooth brush are all that is needed, and by no means are those items essential, except maybe the toothbrush. I've elected to retain the classic B ratings introduced by John Gill for the purposes of this book. Their explanation is as follows:

---

**Standard Bouldering 'B' Ratings**

| | |
|---|---|
| B1- | 5.11a |
| B1 | 5.11 or greater |
| B1+ | 5.12 or greater |
| B2 | 5.13 or greater |
| B3 | Successfully done once, attempted many times. Should problem be repeated, the rating then is considered B2. |

---

This open-endedness reveals the elegance, timelessness and parabolic nature of a thoroughly considered system.

A problem that falls below the rating of B1- will be given a YDS (Yosemite Decimal System, 5.10, 5.9 etc.) rating for its overall difficulty. Keep in mind that all ratings, boulder, topropes or leads, are subjective and can appear easier or more difficult at any given time for any given person. Humidity, fitness, height and mindset can all conspire to affect how one perceives a problem. A partner can be particularly helpful regarding mindset, and can significantly reduce the risk of injury by assisting as a spotter.

*Jeff Sculley succeeds on the very difficult* Gill Problem *on the Red Cross Boulder at Jenny Lake.*

# Jenny Lake Boulders

*"Despite its present deep involvement in developing countries, the
IMF was never intended to be an agency of economic development or
an aid-dispensing institution."*
-Joyce Kolko in her book, Restructuring the World Economy

THESE SCATTERED GRANITE ERRATICS offer about a
dozen problems of varying character and challenge, with
most of the moves falling in the B1 and B1+ range. The one
notable exception, found on the Red Cross boulder, is the
very difficult and overhanging Gill Problem that goes at a
consensus B2. The excellent selection of problems, proximity to Jenny Lake campground and ease of access all add up
to heavy traffic in this area. So if you use chalk, please brush
those holds when you are finished.

**Getting There:** Enter Grand Teton National Park at the
Moose entrance and drive north to the newly expanded Jenny
Lake parking lot. From the parking lot walk west for 100
yards until reaching the bicycle path. Walk north at this point
along the path for 300 yards. Boulders will appear immediately on your left, to the west.

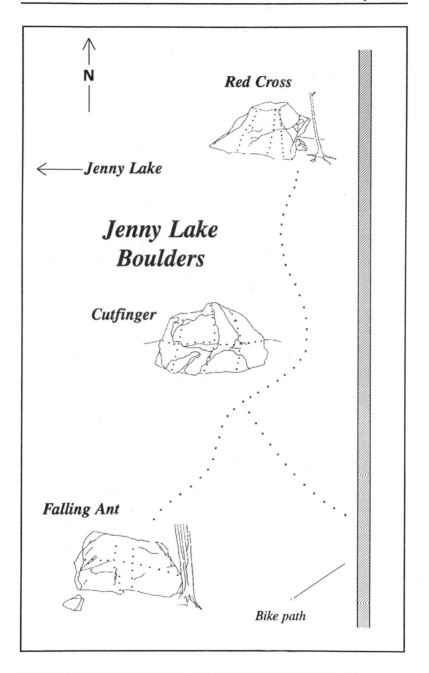

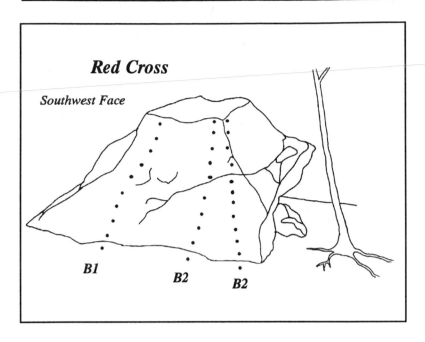

*Red Cross*

*Southwest Face*

B1

B2

B2

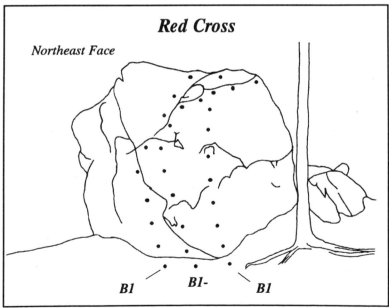

*Red Cross*

*Northeast Face*

B1

B1-

B1

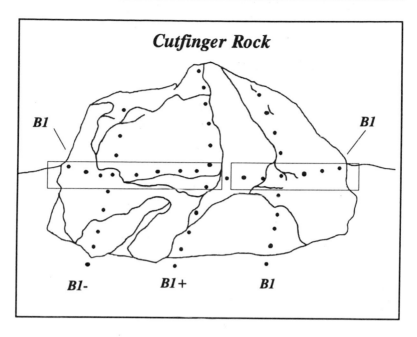

## *Cutfinger Rock*

B1

B1

B1-    B1+    B1

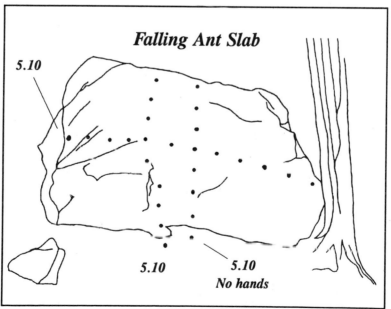

## *Falling Ant Slab*

5.10

5.10    5.10
*No hands*

# *Boulder City*

*"The great democratic danger, according to Tocqueville,*
*is enslavement to public opinion."*
-Allan Bloom in The Closing of the American Mind

**B**OULDER CITY IS A LITTLE-KNOWN bouldering and toprope area within the boundaries of Grand Teton National Park. It consists of a number of granite erratics within a crescent-like moraine whose concave aspect faces north. The difficulty is wide ranging, 5.6—5.12, and many of the taller formations are equipped with toprope anchors. This is an excellent place to take novices. There are six major boulders with approximately thirty different toprope and bouldering problems within a short distance from one another. The character of the problems run from low angle slabs (Boulder #3) to the very overhanging cave-like boulder (Boulder #6) with gneiss/schist bands forming excellent holds. The kettle holes left in the glacier's retreat are sometimes filled with water. Be sure to bring your DEET, Muskcol, Off, or whatever else seems to work.

**Getting There:** Enter GTNP at Moose and drive north to the String Lake/Jenny Lake Loop road. Turn left (west) and follow the winding road to the Cathedral Group turnout. Park here. Continue west on foot along the roadside for 0.2 of a mile, then head north for approximately 300 yards passing a small group of spruce trees on your left. As you approach the moraine, bear left for 100 yards and gain the trail which will lead you over the moraine, which now should be on your right. At the top of the moraine and 20 yards to your right is boulder #1, the tip of which can sometimes be seen from the road, depending upon the light.

While in the area, make plans to have breakfast at least once at the Jenny Lake Lodge. No espresso here, but the regular brew is always hot and fresh. I give it an eight based on *Car Talk's* Café Standards. This is an all-you-can-eat smorgasbord extravaganza with the Cathedral Group looking on—arguably rivals rooftop apple pie at the Bhudda Lodge in Namche.

*Jeff Sculley on a B1- problem on Boulder #1 at Boulder City.*

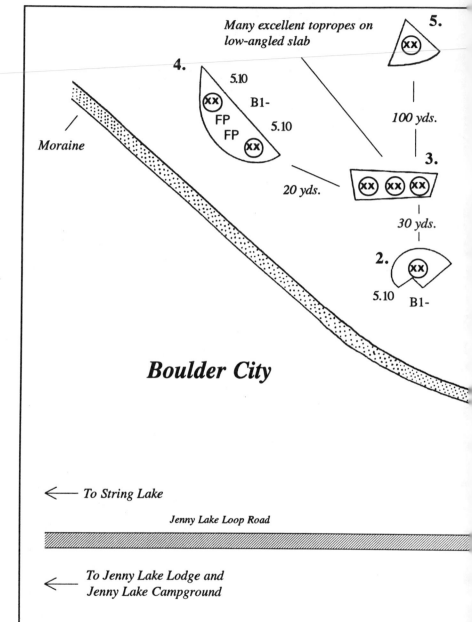

*Many excellent topropes on low-angled slab*

**5.**

**4.**

5.10

B1-

*Moraine*

FP

FP   5.10

*100 yds.*

**3.**

*20 yds.*

*30 yds.*

**2.**

5.10   B1-

**Boulder City**

⟵ *To String Lake*

*Jenny Lake Loop Road*

⟵ *To Jenny Lake Lodge and Jenny Lake Campground*

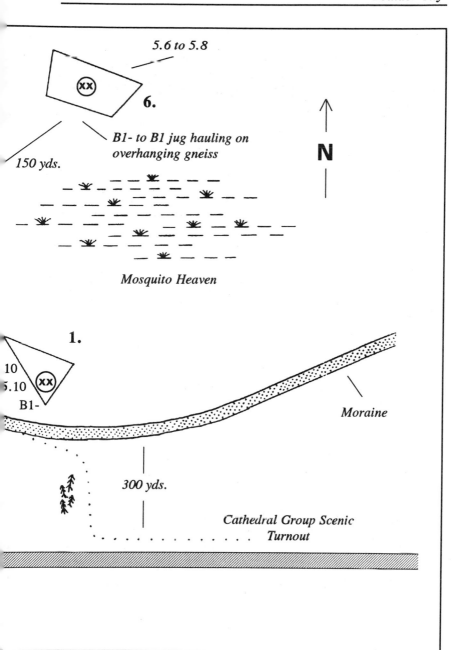

5.6 to 5.8

**6.**

B1- to B1 jug hauling on
overhanging gneiss

150 yds.

Mosquito Heaven

**N**

**1.**

10
5.10
B1-

Moraine

300 yds.

Cathedral Group Scenic
Turnout

*Marjean Heisler on a problem in Section I at Badger Creek.*

# Badger Creek

*"One might consider employment for wages an incredible, albeit necessary, capitalistic hoax. A modern day whoredom with all its impotent trappings."*
-graffiti, Pocatello Unemployment Office

O N THE WEST SIDE OF THE TETONS near the quiet town of Tetonia, Idaho, are the extraordinary Badger Creek Boulders. These boulders are numerous and offer a multitude of problems of varying difficulty. The rock is rhyolite and the long traverses and pocketed overhangs will certainly make the 45 minute drive worth your while. Take note not to climb here if you have a testpiece to attempt the following day. This stuff will destroy your fingers.

What makes Badger so enjoyable, apart from its dramatic location, is the broad offering of problems on very positive holds. Landings are generally safe with maximum height of the boulders about 12 feet. A soft pocket shoe (Ninja, UFO) seems to work best here. The weather is generally milder on this side of the Tetons and early season workouts are usually possible. During the spring, ticks are endemic, and manage to hitch a ride on most every traverse. Mosquitos can be rampant on summer evenings and wasps have a nasty habit of nesting in the pockets late in the summer and in early autumn.

What I've tried to do, topo wise, is give you a rough schematic overview of the area, followed by more specifically detailed drawings of the more concentrated sectors. The sectors, given Roman numerals, represent the upper rim of rhyolite that runs east/west for approximately 300 yards. Independent boulders, numbered in Arabic, are given individual schematic attention and should serve to orient one adequately.

**Getting There:** From Jackson, drive over Teton Pass on US 22 which becomes Scenic 33 in Idaho. One half mile north of Tetonia turn right at the large StorMor silver silo on 300 West. After 2.7 miles turn right on Badger Creek Road. After 0.6 mile, boulders appear on your left, north, fifty yards up a slight incline covered with sagebrush. If you've passed an abandoned tractor on your left, you've gone too far. On your way, you can grab espresso at the Painted Apple Café in Victor and pastry at The Bakery in Driggs.

*Max Yanoff on a B1 problem on Boulder 1.*
*Photo by Marjean Heisler*

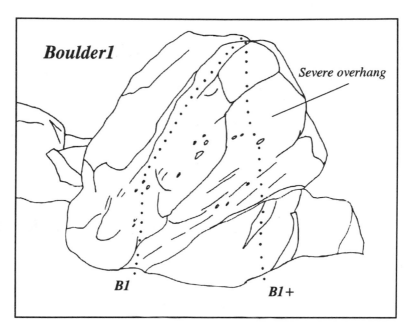

*Boulder1*

Severe overhang

B1

B1+

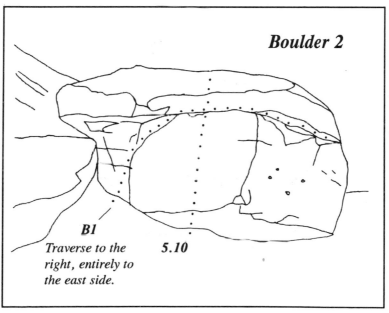

*Boulder 2*

B1

Traverse to the
right, entirely to
the east side.

5.10

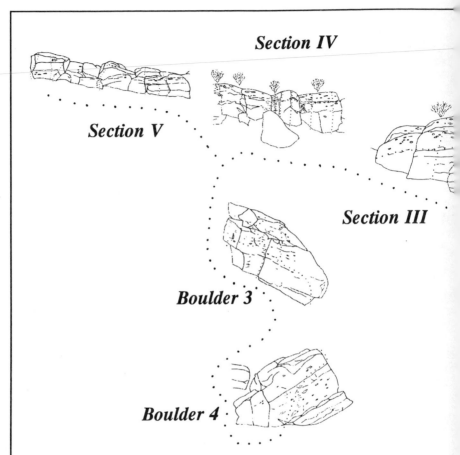

**Section IV**

**Section V**

**Section III**

**Boulder 3**

**Boulder 4**

## *Badger Creek Overview*

*Badger Creek Road*

## Section II

## Section I

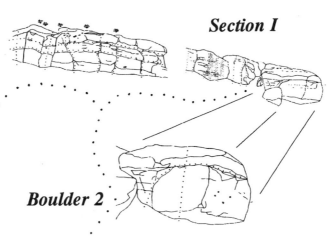

## Boulder 2

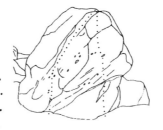

*Boulder 5 is 70 yds. east of Boulder 2.*

N

## Boulder 1

*Trail begins here*

*Parking*

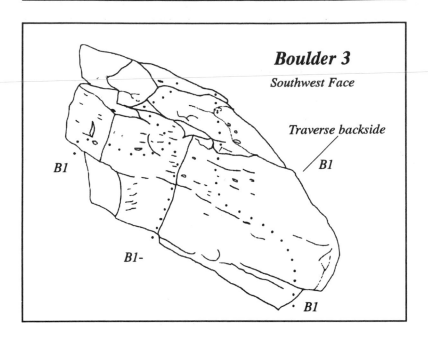

**Boulder 3**

*Southwest Face*

*Traverse backside*

B1

B1

B1-

B1

B1

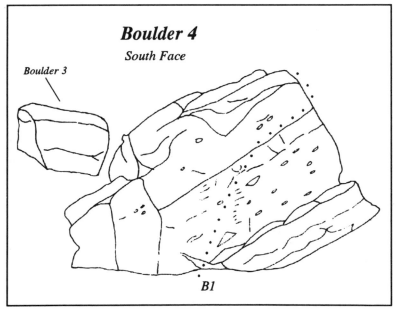

**Boulder 4**

*South Face*

*Boulder 3*

B1

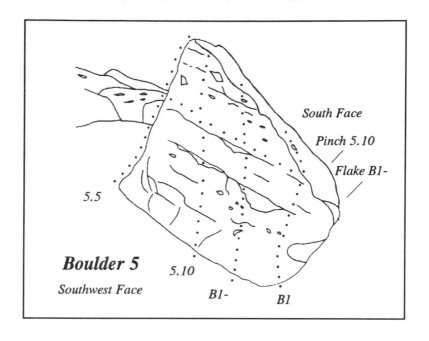

South Face

Pinch 5.10

Flake B1-

5.5

**Boulder 5**

5.10

Southwest Face

B1-

B1

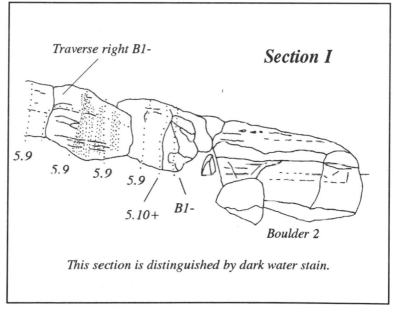

Traverse right B1-

**Section I**

5.9

5.9 5.9 5.9

5.10+ B1-

Boulder 2

*This section is distinguished by dark water stain.*

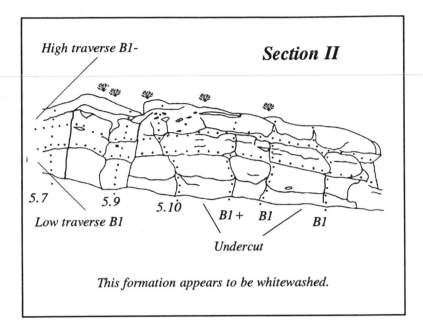

High traverse B1-

**Section II**

5.7  5.9  5.10  B1+  B1  B1

Low traverse B1

Undercut

*This formation appears to be whitewashed.*

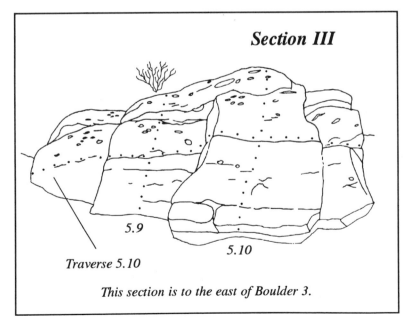

**Section III**

5.9

5.10

Traverse 5.10

*This section is to the east of Boulder 3.*

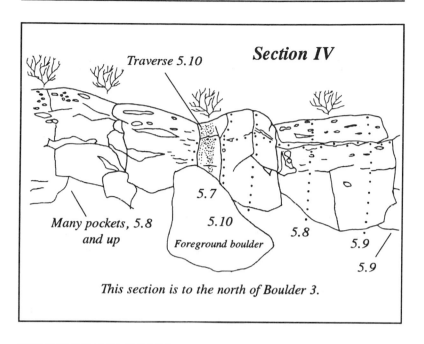

**Section IV**

Traverse 5.10

5.7

5.10

5.8

5.9

5.9

Many pockets, 5.8
and up

Foreground boulder

This section is to the north of Boulder 3.

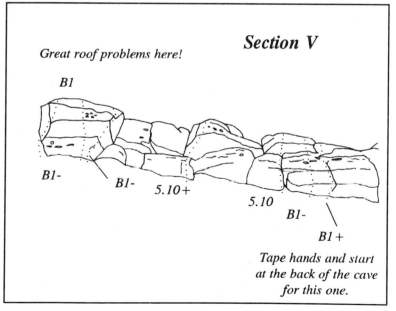

**Section V**

Great roof problems here!

B1

B1-

B1-

5.10+

5.10

B1-

B1+

Tape hands and start
at the back of the cave
for this one.

# *Other Area Crags and Boulders*

**H**ERE ARE SOME BOULDERS that didn't require additional chapters, but are certainly worth your time while in
the area. They are all located within the boundaries of Grand
Teton National Park.

**Other Boulders:** The Corral Boulder, sometimes referred to
as the Taggart Boulder, is behind the corral on the Bradley-
Taggart Lake trail and is directly west of telephone pole #2.
This is a large gneiss boulder with obvious feldspar bands.
The northeast and west aspects offer a half dozen problems
in the 5.10 and B1- range. Be extra careful of your landings
here.

There is also the String Lake Boulder which is found by
crossing the String Lake bridge, located 1.0 mile north from
String Lake Parking area, and turning left following the sign
for Paintbrush Canyon. Walk for 200 yards then turn left
again following a sparse game trail for 75 yards or so. One
should now be standing in front of a 40 foot granite boulder.
The topropes here range from 5.6 to 5.11+. You will need
a moderate rack of medium wired nuts and small Friends to
set the appropriate anchors.

The Boulder Island Boulder is distinguished by a water
approach. A canoe or some other watercraft will be needed.
Check Park regulations for water vehicles. Park at the String
Lake parking area and follow signs directing you to the String
Lake-Leigh Lake portage. At the southern end of Leigh Lake
is an obvious boat landing. Directly in front of you, to the
north, is Boulder Island. Once on the island, the large granite
erratic with the steep west face is the Boulder Island Boulder.

This large boulder (see below) of 60 feet or so, has a wide selection of toprope problems that range from a 5.4 scramble on the east side to a 5.12 tweaker on the west aspect. Don't miss the classic 5.11 finger crack on the west side. The boulder has two sets of bolt anchors for the West Face routes.

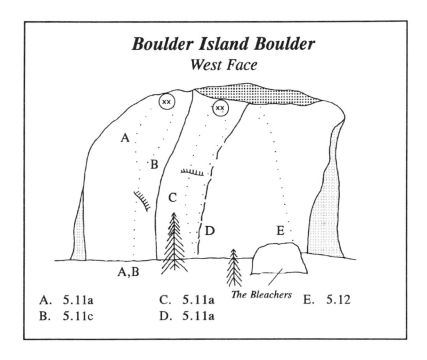

**Boulder Island Boulder**
*West Face*

| | | |
|---|---|---|
| A. 5.11a | C. 5.11a | E. 5.12 |
| B. 5.11c | D. 5.11a | |

*The Bleachers*

**Other Crags:** By all means you must sample the beautiful and delightful climbing of Sinks Canyon just west of Lander, Wyoming, on the lee side of the Wind River Mountains. Only two and a half hours from Jackson Hole is well protected sport climbing on steep dolomite. Pockets, edges and roofs: it is all here. A thorough guide has been written by Greg Collins and a topo map has been designed by Tim Toula. Both publications are useful. The latest update can be found in *Climbing* magazine #129, December 91/Janruary 92, on page 36. Beware: Lander is dry. Your last chance for decent coffee is the Wild West Deli in Duboise.

By now I believe the secret is, quite frankly, hardly a secret any longer. Wild Iris, noted in those ubiquitous **5.10** ads served, intentional or otherwise, as the penultimate Hollywood marketing scam to promote a B-grade movie. Only in this case, Wild Iris sure isn't 'B' material. Referred to by many as the Buoux of the US, these infinite, bulging 100 feet high pocketed dolomite cliffs clearly demonstrate the potential to become a world class sport area. Over a hundred routes are already established at every grade—some go at 5.8, and some are chasing the Maginot Line. The Wild Iris area rests on the high plains just south and west of Lander at the top of South Pass. Topo descriptions and precise directions can be found in *Rock + Ice* issue #48, March/April 1992 in an article by Badaracco, Piana and Hatcher. Additional information and the latest in route development can be gained by stopping at Wild Iris Mountain Sports in Lander. In addition I highly recommend Paul Piana's new guide, *The Legendary Wild Iris* (what's that? marketing?), an eclectic, entertaining and thorough publication.

There is also talk of development on some steep but loose limestone in the Snake River Canyon south of Jackson towards Alpine. Ask around the shops. As of this writing, details were not available.

# Notes of a More General and Needy Nature

*"Dis is not coffee, dis is brown vater!"*
*-from the movie* Baghdad Café

COFFEE, I MEAN, WHAT ELSE IS THERE? And I am at a loss as to what is worse, that brackish stuff most places serve, or none at all. Fortunately, this is not a problem in Jackson. You can find great coffee, espresso, latté and cappucino at both the Shades Café on King Street and at Pearl Street Bagels on, that's right, Pearl Street (near the Post Office and The Cinema). Pearl Street also has the best and widest selection of bagels this side of the Gaza Strip. If you are heading toward Badger Creek or Grand Wall on the west side, get your caffeine fix at The Painted Apple Café in Victor.

Locating housing in Jackson is a nightmare, but camping facilities are in abundance but may be full during peak season (mid-June through late August). Either side of July/August campsites can be found at a number of places. Jenny Lake Campground near the Jenny Lake Ranger Station is often full, but is conveniently located across from the Jenny Lake Boulders. Gros Ventre Campground is a few miles east of Gros Ventre Junction and offers extraordinary views of the entire range. There is a KOA on the Teton Village road and a few RV park/campsites in town. There are more designated sites in the Hoback and Snake River canyons and Jackson is virtually surrounded by National Forest.

There, we've covered the essentials, coffee and sleep. If you find yourself in need of gear, you have quite a wide selection. In Jackson, on the southeast corner of the square (where the elk antler arches are located) is Teton Mountaineering. Across the square on Deloney Street is Skinny Skis. At Dornan's, near the Moose entrance to GTNP, is Moosely Seconds.

If, for some unexpected and unfortunate reason, gravity surprises you and a sudden meeting with the earth occurs, Jackson has an excellent array of emergency services. All these agencies can be reached by dialing 911. The county has EMS, Jackson Hole Air Ambulance, Teton County Sheriff, Jackson Police and the widely known and well respected Jenny Lake Climbing Rangers. For minor emergencies there is Emerg + A + Care of Jackson Hole one mile west of town in the Powderhorn Mall and Insta-Care a half mile west of town across from Albertsons. For illness or injury of a more severe nature, there is St. John's Hospital approximately one mile east of the town square on East Broadway.

Oh, almost forgot. Food! Food is important, even to sport climbers. If you share the concept of supporting the local economy, Fred's Market is the choice for groceries. They are located in downtown Jackson across from Mountain Camera, Dynamic Health, and the laundromat. If you must have airconditioning and fifty aisles from which to choose, there is an Albertsons a few blocks further west.

If you wish to get away from the booming metropolis that Jackson is quickly becoming, spend a night or two at the Climber's Ranch in Grand Teton National Park. Sponsored by the American Alpine Club and expertly run and hosted by Ron and Ruth Matous, these lodgings offer sleeping quarters and shared kitchen facilities at the foot of the Tetons. An exellent evironment to meet others and get updated information on the ever changing condidtions in the mountains. Call 307-733-7271 for more information.

# YDS/French
# Conversion Table

| | | | |
|---|---|---|---|
| 5.9 | 5+ | 5.12a/b | 7b |
| 5.9+ | 6a | 5.12b | 7b |
| 5.10a | 6a | 512b/c | 7b+ |
| 5.10a/b | 6a | 5.12c | 7c |
| 5.10b | 6a+ | 5.12c/d | 7c |
| 5.10b/c | 6b | 5.12d/13a | 7c |
| 5.10c | 6b | 5.13a | 7c+ |
| 5.10c/d | 6b | 5.13a/b | 8a |
| 5.10d | 6b+ | 5.13b | 8a |
| 5.10d/11a | 6c | 5.13b/c | 8a |
| 5.11a | 6c | 5.13c | 8a |
| 5.11a/b | 6c | 5.13c/d | 8a+ |
| 5.11b | 6c | 5.13d/14a | 8b |
| 5.11b/c | 6c+ | 5.14a | 8b |
| 5.11c | 7a | 5.14a/b | 8b |
| 5.11c/d | 7a | 5.14b | 8b+ |
| 5.11d/12a | 7a+ | 5.14b/c | 8c |
| 5.12a | 7b | 5.14c | 8c |

# *Recommended Climbs*

**Blacktail Butte**

Do the Right Thing  5.11d
The Water Streak  5.12b
Time Flies While You're
    Alive  5.10c

**Upper Blacktail**

Muy Macho  5.10d
Graceland  5.11b

**Hoback Shield**

A Thousand Cranes  5.9
Electric Shower  5.11b
Dengue Fever  5.10d
Fandango  5.10c
La Bamba  5.10a

**Rodeo Wall**

Bulldog  5.11b
Buck Dancer  5.10c
Betty Tendonblaster  5.9

**Grand Wall**

Arms Deal  5.13a
Dr. Hole  5.12a
Bambi  5.11a
Mayday  5.12a

**The Tram**   S&S

   Corbet's
   West

Shadow Silence  5.10b
Fire in the Hole  5.10c
Renaissance    5.13
Turbulence    5.11b
Sound Chaser  5.11c

| The Tram | Corbet's East | Saxifrage 5.9 |
| | | Sky Pilot 5.11c |
| | | Nature Hike 5.10d |
| | | Ravin' Roof Bypass 5.12a |
| **Heise** | | Hanging Humor 5.10d |
| | | The Devil and Miss Jones 5.10b |
| | | Rock-a-Bye Baby 5.9 |
| | | Dark Justice 5.12b |
| | | The Bitter End 5.11d |
| **Paramount** | | Aerial Boundaries 5.9 |
| | | Take the Heise Plunge 5.10d |
| | | Chuck & Jed's Excellent Adventure 5.8 |
| | | Positively Negative 5.11a |

# Climbs Catagorized
# by Rating

*"Without measurement, there can be no effective practice."*
*-Eugene Michels*

## 5.8

**Hoback Shield**
> A. Toprope
> Malvado Edge
> The Bulge
> Deception, 2nd pitch

**Paramount**
> Chuck & Jed's Excellent
>     Adventure
> Mr. Roger's Neighborhood
> Wild Thing
> Fly by Night

## 5.9

**Blacktail Butte**
> Right Crack
> Raven Crack

**Hoback Shield**
> A Thousand Cranes
> Malvado Edge, 2nd pitch
> Muffbuster, 2nd pitch
> The Hunter—poor pro on lower moves
> Patty's Butt
> Hookit
> Jam or Slam
> Bolt Face

# 5.9 cont.

**The Tram—Corbet's East**
    Saxifrage
    Grey-Crowned Cracks

**Rodeo Wall**
    Betty Tendonblaster
    Thelma

**Heise**
    Pigeon Crack
    Rock-a-Bye Baby

**Paramount**
    Aerial Boundaries
    Fantasy

# 5.10

**Blacktail/Upper Blacktail**
    Time Flies While You're Alive
    Muy Macho

**Hoback Shield**
    Petzle Logic
    The Joker
    Muffbuster, 1st pitch
    Electric Shower, 2nd pitch
    She's Gotta' Have It!
    Dengue Fever
    Fandango
    Naughty Guides
    La Bamba
    Mc Flatus Roof
    The Bulge, 2nd pitch
    Deception, 1st pitch

**The Tram—S&S**
    Shadow Silence

New World
Fire in the Hole
**The Tram—Corbet's East**
Nature Hike
**Rodeo Wall**
Ten Second Ride
Buck Dancer
Copenhagen
I Against I
Louise
**Grand Wall**
S.O.S.
**Heise**
Hanging Humor
The Devil and Miss Jones
Tradmania
**Paramount**
Thin Red Line
Take the Heise Plunge
Farr Side
Dark Side

# 5.11

**Backtail Butte/Upper Blacktail**
As You Wish
Inconceivable
Do the Right Thing
Bolt Route
Diagonal Crack
Graceland
Wild at Heart
Blitzkrieg
**Hoback Shield**
Electric Shower, 1st pitch

# 5.11 cont.

Nhervus Sheep
Nhervus Sheep Direct
Y. ?

**The Tram—Corbet's West**

Turbulence
Sound Chaser

**The Tram—Corbet's East**

Harebell
Sky Pilot
Ravin' Roof Bypass—eliminate last move

**Rodeo Wall**

Bulldog
Cowgirls Wear Chaps Only

**Grand Wall**

Munger Crack
Ladykiller
Bambi
Thumper
Kin-Jite
Ninjitsu

**Heise**

Retro Man
Born to Rock
H. Toprope
Clip Me Deadly
Equilibrium
The Bitter End

**Paramount**

Positively Negative

# 5.12

**Blacktail Butte/Upper Blacktail**
Water Streak
The Arch
Arch Direct
Jingus Road
Kehoe Kling
Your Route
Breashear's Route
**The Tram—Corbet's West**
Shining Path
**The Tram—Corbet's East**
Ravin' Roof Bypass
Ravin' Roof
**Grand Wall**
Dr. Hole
Mayday
High Noon
Afternoon Delight
Uki-Waza
**Heise**
Dark Justice
Wicked Cave
If You See a Trad...

# 5.13

**Blacktail Butte/Upper Blacktail**
Water Streak Direct
**The Tram—Corbet's West**
Renaissance
**Grand Wall**
Arms Deal
**Heise**
Rock Ninja—toprope

# *Notes*

# Some Useful Phone Numbers

| | |
|---|---|
| **Emergencies** | **911** |
| Climber's Ranch in GTNP | 1-307-733-7271 |
| **Columbine: Active Sportswear** | **733-7179** |
| **Emerg+A+Care** | **733-8002** |
| **Exum School of Mountaineering** | **733-2297** |
| Grand Teton National Park | 733-2880 |
| GTNP—camping and weather | 733-2220 |
| **Highway Patrol** | **1-800-442-9090** |
| Hoback Sports | 733-5335 |
| **Instacare** | **733-7003** |
| Jack Dennis' Outdoor Shop | 733-3270 |
| Jackson Hole Mountain Guides | 733-4979 |
| **Moosely Seconds** | **733-7176** |
| Mountain Bike Outfitters | 733-3314 |
| **Pearl Street Bagels** | **739-1218** |
| **Police** | **733-1430** |
| Post Office | 733-3650 |
| Road and Weather | 733-9966 |
| **Scott's Ski & Sports, Pocatello, Id.** | **208-232-1449** |
| Shades Café | 733-2015 |
| **Sheriff** | **733-4052** |
| **Skinny Skis** | **733-6094** |
| **St. John's Hospital** | **733-3636** |
| **Technical Sports** | **733-2471** |
| Teton Mountaineering | 733-3595 |
| Teton Rock Gym | 733-0707 |
| Teton Cyclery | 733-4386 |
| Wild Iris Mtn. Sports, Lander, Wy. | 1-332-4541 |
| Yellowstone National Park | 1-543-2575 |

# Regional Books of Interest

*A Climber's Guide to the Teton Range (Vols. I & II)* by
     Leigh Ortenberger and Renny Jackson
*Teton Classics* by Richard Rossiter
*Creation of the Teton Landscape* by David Love
*Yellowstone Trails* by Mark C. Marschall
*Field Book to Yellowstone Park and the Absoroka Range*
     by Bonney and Bonney
*50 Ski Tours in Jackson Hole and Yellowstone* by
     Richard Dumais
*Climbing and Hiking in the Wind River Mountains*
     by Joe Kelsey (rumors of a new edition soon)
*Wind River Trails* by Finis Mitchell
*Season of the Elk* by Dan Krakle
*Field Book to The Wind River Range* by Bonney and
     Bonney
*Bonney's Guide to GTNP & Jackson Hole* by
     Lorraine Bonney
*Birds of Grand Teton National Park* by Bert
     Raynes
*Plants of Yellowstone and Grand Teton Park* by R.
     Shaw
*Grand Teton Photographer's Guide* by Leo Larson
*Grand Teton Handbook* by the National Park Service
*Traveler's Guide to the Geology of Wyoming* by
     D.L. Blackstone
*Ecology of Jackson Hole* by Tim Clark
*The Grand Controversy* by Lorraine Bonney

Many outdoor retailers, primarily Teton Mountaineering, Skinny Skis and Jack Dennis, carry a wide selection of USGS 7.5' and 15' topographical maps for northwestern Wyoming as well as for the Wind River Mountains. For convenience and value, I recommend the Earthwalk Press series of maps for Grand Teton National Park, Yellowstone National Park and the Wind River Mountains by Leo and Helen Larson.

# *Glossary*

*"Languages have in them a certain life force, and certain powers of
absorption and growth. But they can decay and they can die."*
*-George Steiner*

**Barndoor:** when the body insists on swinging right or left away from
the rock as if one's hand and/or foot is a hinge.

**Beta:** information, either verbal or through observation, regarding a
route in the form of esoteric moves, obscure sequences, difficult
clips, hidden holds etc.

**Big Air:** a long fall.

**Bolt to Bolt:** working a route on lead, usually resting at each bolt.

**Chopped:** a route in which the bolts have been removed, generally
not by the party who put them in.

**Choss:** poor quality rock.

**Clip-up:** a route where bolts and hangers are permanently placed and
only quickdraws are needed for protection.

**Deck:** when the body falls to the ground, usually the result of the
second bolt being too high above the first. Generally frowned
upon in the sport climbing world.

**Dogging:** the act of resting on protection.

**Draws:** a short runner, usually sewn, no longer than six inches and
equipped at each end with a carabiner.

**Deadpoint:** the uppermost point when the body is momentarily
motionless during a lunge, also referred to as the apex.

**Enhancement:** to alter a hold in such a manner as to make it more
useful (clean loose material, file sharp edges, epoxy loose
essential holds, etc.).

**Equipped:** same as clip-up (French).

**Flag:** a means of counterbalancing with the leg which then allows a
particular hand-hold to become useful. Can also be used to
prevent a barndoor effect.

**Flash:** a successful ascent of a route, on one's first attempt, without
prior knowledge.

**Good pump:** as in getting a 'good pump.' A good work-out.

**Grounder:** 1. a ball hit on the ground to the infield 2. same as deck.

**Hangdog:** one who rests on protection.

**Hanging:** same as dogging.

**I'm off!:** 1. climber is clipped into the anchors or otherwise secure and can be safely taken off belay. 2. climber is about to fall or is already in the act of falling. The difference between meanings can generally be detected in the inflection. In all seriousness, as you can well imagine, some frightening falls have taken place because of this dual meaning. Get this straight with your partner beforehand.

**Lunge:** to actually leap for the next hold.

**Onsight:** a successful ascent without prior knowledge (beta).

**Pinkpoint:** a successful ascent with prior knowledge and quickdraws or natural protection already in place. A term falling out of vogue since most cutting edge leads are attempted with draws in place.

**Pro:** protection, i.e.. bolts, nuts, pitons, etc.

**Pumped:** a tight, useless feeling in the forearms just prior to failure (time to shake out).

**Quickdraw:** same as draw.

**Rap:** rappel

**Redpoint:** a successful ascent of a route when one has prior knowledge either in the form of a previous attempt or has received beta.

**Rockover:** the instance when after a high step, one then proceeds to shift the body's weight entirely over that foot. Will sometimes be heard as 'rock left' or 'rock right' during a beta session.

**Screamer:** a particularly exciting fall.

**Shake out:** to lower the arms and shake them as a means of increasing circulation and reducing fatigue.

**Sketch:** loss of form during a climb. First phase of flailing.

**Stack:** to arrange the rope in such a way to ensure that it will run freely when fed to the lead climber. Particularly important if difficult clips are anticipated. 2. to use any combination of fingers, hands or fists to allow them to fit more securely in a crack.

**Static:** to reach a hold in full control of the body, unlike a lunge or throw.

**Stick:** as in 'Stick it!' A successful lunge or throw.

**Stick-clip:** because of the sustained difficulty of the opening moves, the first clip is relatively high off the ground and is made with the assistance of a long stick or something similar before one starts climbing.

**Take:** belayer is to take in slack and hold the climber. Used often when working a route.

**Throw:** to reach a hold as the result of rapid upward momentum. One may not actually leave the rock as in a lunge. See also; deadpoint.

**Toast:** as in 'I'm toast,' same as pumped.

**TR:** toprope.

**Whipper:** same as big air.

**Working a Route:** practicing the moves on a route in preparation for the red point.

**You're on:** climber is being safely belayed.

**Suggested readings:** *Beyond Culture* by Edward T. Hall and *Language and Silence* by George Steiner

# *Index*

# About This Book

*"The bio-chip, once implanted in the brain, will be capable of storing the entire Library of Congress."*
*-from* The History of the Future *by Lorie and Murray-Clark*

THIS HAS BEEN ONE OF THE MOST challenging, frustrating, and rewarding projects I have ever completed. It involved more work than I imagined and involved less sleep than I had hoped. With that said, if there is anyone out there contemplating such an undertaking, I encourage you and recommend it highly. What follows are some tips I gleaned as a neophyte desktop publisher. I hope you find them useful. Suggestions are based on the use of an IBM/PC compatible.

Unlike that extraordinary computer located between our ears, you can simply add memory to your desktop computer. I've found you'll need at least 40 megabytes (megs) of hard drive (hd) to accommodate graphics and 4 megs of RAM (random access memory). The pros prefer 6 to 8 megs of RAM. Microsoft recommends 2 megs to run *Windows 3.0,* but I found, when multitasking in the desktop, that occasional crashes occurred even with 4 megs. And besides, whoever complained of having too much memory?

Again, Microsoft suggests a 286 cpu (central processing unit). Forget it. Go no less than a 386sx to ensure the speed required so you do not forget what project you were working on as the system searches for the next program. Speaking of programs, I used *Aldus PageMaker 4.0 for Windows* for page layout. After using *Ami' Pro* by Samna for the first edition, I found *PageMaker* to be **much** more intuitive and user friendly. I am not alone. It just won the Reader's Choice Award in *Publish!*, December 1991, for Macs and PCs. Other than the technical information, throw away the how-to manuals supplied with *PageMaker* and purchase *Real World PageMaker* by Berst, Roth, Kvern and Dunn, published by Bantam. It is by far the best, and is even fun to read.

If at all possible, go straight to a laser printer—do not pass Go. With today's prices, you may even consider Postscript (you'll want it eventually). By doing so, you can print camera-ready copy in your home. If you own a dot printer you can print-to-disk if you have the correct printer drivers installed, in which case your camera-ready will be printed out-of-house, but you never get the feel for the final product this way. I found this to be essential in making the numerous corrections required. Better yet, get a modem and let your fingers do the walking. In the comfort of your own home you can proof your work until the cows come home or your Hilti battery recharges. Your files, preferably printed to Post-script, can then be transferred via phoneline to a Service Bureau and printed upwards of 2400 dpi (dots per inch). The difference between 300 dpi (standard laser printer resolution) and 2400 dpi (Linotype Typesetter, Linotronic 300, Agfa Compugraphic) is astonishing.*

Buy more kitchenware and paper plates. Once up and running you'll burn pots and never do the dishes, if, of course, you ever did them.

Read, read, read. Do a Michener and go to the library and pull every book you can find on graphics, publishing, book production and design. Make friends with folks in the business. They are proud of their work, give new meaning to detail and have a deep appreciation for the historical signifi-cance of publishing. Their enthusiasm is contagious and helpfulness immeasurable. Once again it was made clear how little I know.

Finally, and probably most important, find a niche where no book currently resides, secure someone you trust as an editor and go to work.

---

* the current commercial standard is 1000 dpi in most lithographic print houses.

---